This Book Belongs To:

_____

This book has additional free resources available:

Parent Guide,
Coloring Sheets,
and More to Come!

Check out the website for more information!
Sunnyfieldhealing.com/Georges-adventures

George Learns About Mindfulness

Author: Mikki Mason
Illustrator: Tincho Schmidt

"I'm so upset right now!" George exclaimed. "My brother always gets his way, I just don't know what to do! Mom told me I need to calm down, but I just don't know how!"

George saw his best friend, Henry, the goat by the barn. "Henry, I am so mad at my brother but I don't know how to calm down!" George fumed.

"Well George, follow me. I will show you how my friends cool down," Henry replied.

"Let's look at my friends, the ducks. If they need to calm down, they start quacking their favorite song, like we sing our favorite songs," Henry stated.

"I have a favorite song!" George exclaimed. "I will join them with my favorite song!"

What is your favorite song to sing?

"When the pigs need to relax, they lay down and meditate by taking deep breaths in the mud," Henry explained.

"I don't have to lay in the mud, do I Henry?" George wondered.

Henry laughed, "Let's not get muddy quite yet! We can join them in the grass, lay down like they do and take a few deep breaths."

Can you do some deep breaths with George and Henry?

Henry explained "Cows like to practice eating healthy to keep their mind clear."

"I like eating healthy!" George exclaimed. "My favorite healthy snack to eat is carrots! When I get to eat carrots, I feel calm and happy."

What is your favorite kind of healthy snack that keeps your mind clear?

"Horses also love practicing mindfulness by clearing their heads while they trot around," Henry reported. "Exercise can help calm your mind when you feel upset."

"I can't trot, but I can sure run fast," George beamed. "I'm going to race him Henry, will you judge who gets back here first?"

"I'm ready George, on your mark, get set, go!," Henry cheered.

Can you trot around like a horse?

"Look Henry, my cat looks like he is doing some funny poses," George stated.

"George, they are doing yoga poses. Yoga is a great way to stretch out your body and to help refocus your brain," Henry stated. "Let's join him by doing some yoga of our own. Be careful though, don't get stuck in your pose!"

Can you practice some yoga with Henry and George?

"Sheep also have a way to calm down, and that's by counting," Henry reported.

"What do they usually count to calm down Henry?" George questioned.

"Why George, they count themselves!" Henry praised

"I like to count how many stuffed animals are in my room," George offered.

"Those are great things to count George. Let's count how many sheep we see here." Henry stated.

How many sheep are on the farm?

"George, I think your dog has the next thing to do when you need to calm down," Henry volunteered. "She is playing with her toys, and it looks like she wants to play fetch with you."

"I love playing fetch with Sheena. Watch how far I can throw the ball for her." George beamed.

Is there someone that you can play ball with?

"George, you can also just sit and practice gratitude for everything around you," Henry said. "My favorite is sitting and watching the sunset, enjoying being outside and taking a few deep breaths of fresh air."

George sighed "That sounds so relaxing Henry and I love all the colors in the sunset."

Where is your favorite place to sit and practice gratitude ?

"The last thing you can try George, is to give your family a big hug," Henry encouraged. "Getting a big hug from your family can help you calm down and help you feel happy again."

"I love big hugs Henry. They make me feel safe and secure." George blushed.

Do you like getting big hugs from your family?

Try giving your family a big hug now!

"Henry, I feel so much better now," George beamed. "Thank you for showing me different ways to become calm."

"You're welcome, George!" Henry exclaimed.

Henry reminded his friend once more, "Next time you feel sad or mad George, try using the different skills you learned today to help you feel better."

"I will," George smiled. "I have learned so much today and I cannot wait to try them all again!"

George wants to know what skill was your favorite that you want to try?

The End.

Mikki is a mental health professional who is passionate in working with children and saw a need for additional resources. She is an advocate for children and hopes that you enjoy the start of a great adventure when it comes to talking about children's mental health.

Visit her website for more information about the author and additional resources that go with the book!

Sunnyfieldhealing.com/Georges-adventures

CPSIA information can be obtained
at www.ICGtesting.com
Printed in the USA
BVHW061152261120
594139BV00002B/12